Old Ironsides Activity Book

Illustrations by Stephen Biesty

Text by Richard Platt and the USS Constitution Museum

A project of the USS Constitution Museum, Boston

2012

USS Constitution Museum

Project Director
Sarah H. Watkins

Project Manager
Rebecca Parmer

Design by Margaret Mazz and Jon Christensen

Project Team
Matthew Brenckle, Jon Christensen, Rebecca Crawford, Gary Foreman, Jessica Fretts,
Hillary Richmond Goodnow, Tegan Kehoe, Robert Kiihne, Margaret Mazz,
Rebecca Parmer, Anne Grimes Rand, Chris Schrepel and Sarah Watkins

Special thanks to all the staff, volunteers, and interns of the USS Constitution Museum
who helped in the creation of the Old Ironsides Activity Book.

The USS Constitution Museum is especially indebted to Stephen Biesty and Richard Platt
for their unparalleled enthusiasm and support of this project.

Development of the Old Ironsides Activity Book was made possible through federal
funds provided by the Institute of Museum and Library Services and administered by
the Massachusetts Board of Library Commissioners.

ISBN 978-0-615-59898-7

Welcome aboard!

Prepare to set sail on a seafaring adventure. Explore the life of a young sailor on board USS *Constitution*, "Old Ironsides," during the War of 1812 from recruiting to battle to victorious homecoming. Tie a knot, try a sailor's recipe, tell a tall tale, and test your courage in battle.

Meet the crew and discover life on board *Constitution*'s crowded decks through vivid, detailed drawings, lively text, museum artifacts, hands-on activities, and online games.

This book and its accompanying website www.asailorslifeforme.org draw on a decade of intensive research by the USS Constitution Museum to offer the most accurate and thrilling depiction of life at sea ever presented.

Now raise the anchors and sail into the War of 1812!

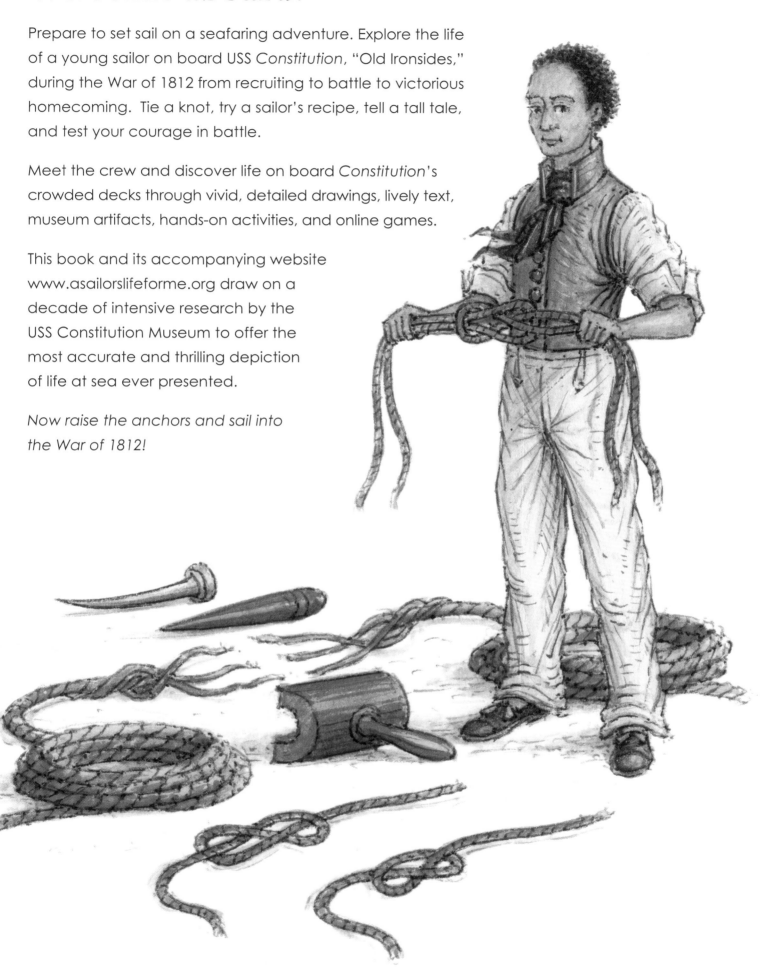

Hands-On Activities

JOIN THE CREW

Join the Crew

Answer the recruiter's questions to see if a sailor's life is for you. On a separate piece of paper, keep a tally of your "yes" answers, and then see where you rank in *Constitution*'s crew.

1 & 2: Have you ever swung in a hammock? Are you willing to sleep next to 200 of your closest friends who badly need baths?

Ships are crowded places. There is no way to escape the sounds and smells of your shipmates.

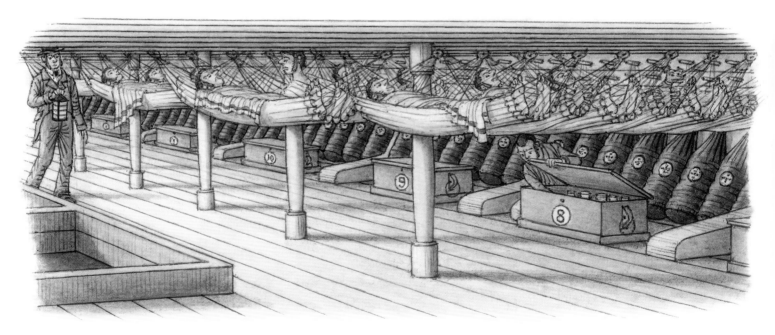

3 & 4: Do you have all of your teeth? Do you have all your fingers and toes?

A sailor must move quickly and learn to tie many knots – hard to do without fingers and toes.

5: Are you willing to eat biscuit as hard as a brick?

At sea, sailors eat hard bread called ship's biscuit. They dunk it in their stew to make it easier to chew.

6: Are you healthy and free from scurvy, rickets or gout?

There is no place in the Navy for sick sailors. Yet the lack of fresh food on board makes many of them ill.

7: Are you afraid of heights?

Sailors must climb high up the masts and balance on a thin rope while they haul in heavy sails.

Quiz scoring summary:

0–2: You're better off ashore, mate! But I'm short of recruits, and I will take you on if you promise to shape up.

3–5: I've seen worse, so welcome to the Navy. Be sure not to step out of line, though.

6–7: Hey, you are a natural sailor! Are you sure you have never been to sea before? I'm proud to have you aboard.

Did you know?

A Sailor:

- Enlists for two years
- Joins a specific ship
- No height requirement
- No age restriction
- Must know how to hand, reef and steer
- Must buy own clothes
- Pay for Ordinary Seaman: $8-10/month
- Pay for Able Seaman: $12/month

A Marine:

- Enlists for five years
- Joins the Corps of Marines
- Must be 5 ft 6 in or taller (except musicians)
- Must be between 18 and 40
- A soldier at sea, doesn't need sailing experience
- Receives an eye-catching uniform
- Pay for Marine Private: $6/month

Which would you rather be?

Why did men join *Constitution*'s crew during the War of 1812?

There was a range of motivations, including:

- The need for a job
- Advance wages
- Limited options ashore
- Owing money to someone, such as a landlord
- Livelihood interrupted by the War
- Prize money (extra pay for successful battles)
- Desire for adventure and an active life
- Family tradition
- Buddies signing on
- Reputation of the Captain
- Patriotism

In My Own Words

"After having been kept so long in suspense it is like emancipation from slavery to have my name enrolled on the list of this gallant crew and be permitted to serve my country in a ship which has already so eminently distinguished herself..."

- Pardon Mawney Whipple, 1813

JOIN THE CREW

THE REAL THING

> MIRROR-OFFICE, June 22, 1812.
>
> ## WAR DECLARED!!
>
> Extract of a Letter from Washington, received in this City, dated June 18, 1812.
>
> " The injunction of secrecy is just removed. An act has passed, and been approved by the President, declaring —THAT WAR EXISTS BETWEEN THE KINGDOM OF GREAT-BRITAIN AND IRELAND AND THEIR DEPEN-DENCIES, AND THE UNITED STATES OF AMERI-CA; *and also authorizing the President to employ the land and naval force to carry it on, and to issue Letters of Marque and Reprisal.*"
>
> In the House of Representatives—Yeas 79, Nays 49, majority for War 30; Senate—Yeas 19, Noes 13, majority 6.
>
> ---
>
> *From the New-York Evening Post of Saturday last.*
>
> Brigadier-General BLOOMFIELD, commander of the United States' forces on this station, received a letter by a government Express from the Secre-tary at War, this morning, and immediately issued the following :—
>
> (COPY.)
>
> " GENERAL ORDERS.
>
> " HEAD-QUARTERS, 20th June, 1812.
>
> " General Bloomfield announces to the troops that " WAR IS DECLAR-ED BY THE UNITED STATES AGAINST GREAT-BRITAIN."
>
> " By ORDER,
>
> " R. H. MACPHERSON, Aid-de-Camp."
>
> Government Expresses passed through this city, about 10 o'clock for Albany and Boston, with the above intelligence.

In 1812, America declared war against its old enemy, Great Britain. The young nation defended its right to trade freely and protested the offensive British practice of plucking sailors from American ships and forcing them to sail under the British flag. Notices like this were posted for all to see to help spread the word that the country was at war.

Thousands of these broadsides were printed in 1812, but this fragile, ragged poster is one of the few that have survived.

"War Declared!!" Broadside, 1812
Collection of the USS Constitution Museum, Boston

JOIN THE CREW

Who am I?

I'm Dorothea. I work as a servant in the Robert household in Brookhaven, New York. After I married William Cooper, a member of the Unkechaug tribe of Long Island, the Robert family employed my husband on their farm. We've got two little girls, Charlotte and Fanny.

THE **REAL** THING

Sailor's Seabag

What would you bring to entertain and comfort you while separated from your family and friends for so long?

Space on board ship was extremely limited. Sailors had to fit all their belongings into a small bag like this one owned by John Lord. After packing the clothes required there was little space left for reminders of home.

Seabag owned by John Lord, early 19th century
Lord was Gunner on board *Constitution* from 1824-1828
Collection of the USS Constitution Museum, Boston

Decorate Your Seabag

Draw a seabag like the one pictured here and decorate it with some of your favorite things.

Or, design a bag online. Click on the "Hands-on Activities" link on www.asailorslifeforme.org.

To pack clothing and personal items for your two-year enlistment, click on the "Hands-on Activities" link on www. asailorslifeforme.org.

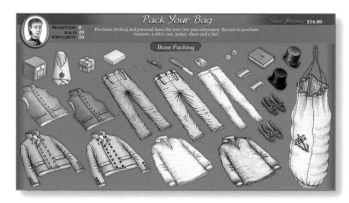

Make a Paper Boat (Easy)

Sailors left their lives on land behind for a life of adventure at sea. Separated from family and friends ashore, sailors considered the ship, home, and their shipmates, family.

Try your hand at origami, the ancient Japanese art of paper folding, to create a model of the sailors' home afloat.

Step 1	
Fold a square piece of paper in half and open it back up. Cut the paper in half along the crease.	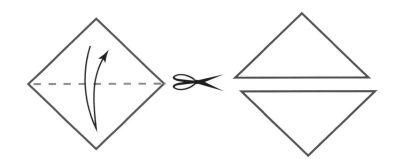
Step 2	
Fold one of the triangles in half and open it back up.	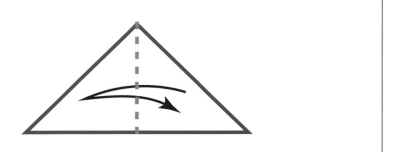

Step 3	
Fold the top corner down to meet the bottom of the triangle.	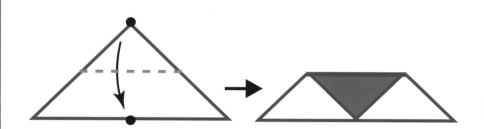
Step 4	
Fold the two bottom corners up to meet together in the middle.	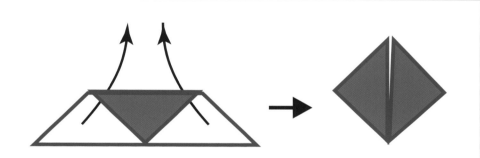
Step 5	
Fold the bottom corner up to the center of the model. Then turn the model over.	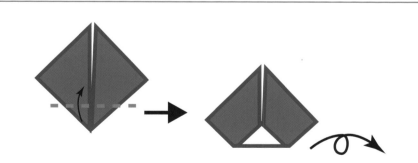

Congratulations!
You've completed your boat.
Now you can decorate it.

Make a Paper Boat (Harder)

Step 1 Fold a piece of rectangular paper in half and open it back up.	
Step 2 Fold the paper in half towards the bottom.	
Step 3 Fold the corners down to the center.	
Step 4 Fold the bottom of the front layer up. Turn the paper over and fold the other bottom up.	

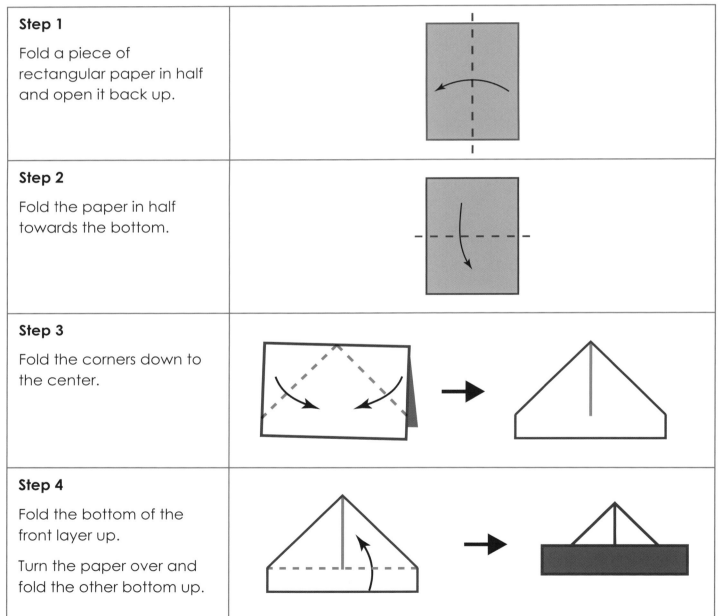

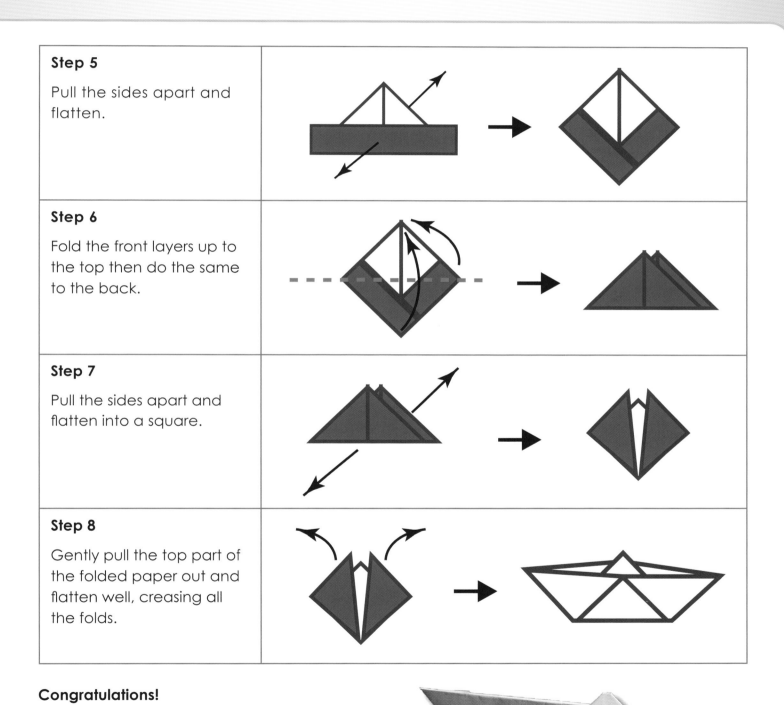

Step 5

Pull the sides apart and flatten.

Step 6

Fold the front layers up to the top then do the same to the back.

Step 7

Pull the sides apart and flatten into a square.

Step 8

Gently pull the top part of the folded paper out and flatten well, creasing all the folds.

Congratulations!
You've completed your boat.
Now you can decorate it.

How would you feel if you or a loved one left home for two years?

"It appears to me at present that a man must be happy who sacrifices everything for his country. My ambition leads me this way, and should I be so fortunate as to prove serviceable to my country, I shall be in the zenith of my glory."

- Pardon Mawney Whipple, 1813

"My parting was ... a mixture of hopes and fears, of tears and smiles, of sunshine and cloud."

-Samuel Leech, 1810

"I leaned over the taffrail and gazed on the departing boat -with mother on board-, and when it disappeared, I turned away and wept."

- Samuel Leech, 1810

"I continue to feel as cheerful as our separation would admit - I will not, indulge myself with gloomy fears - but anticipate the pleasures your safe return will certainly produce."

-Abby Chew, 1813

"We have both felt and expressed the greatest anxiety, in the present state of affairs his post must be a hazardous one...."

- Elizabeth Hull, 1812

"Towards night, my mother left me; it scarcely need be said, she wept when we parted. What mother would not?"

- Samuel Leech, 1810

"It is only those that are blessed with an affectionate mother that can appreciate my feelings at taking leave of her."

-Isaac Mayo, 1809

THE REAL THING

I _Jesse Cole Seaman_ on board the United States vessel of war _Constitution_ commanded by _Silas Talbot Esqr_ do by these presents allot _eight Dollars fifty Cents_ per month of my wages for the support of my family. And I do hereby appoint _Tabitha my Wife_ my Attorney to receive for that purpose from the Navy Agent at the port of _Boston_ the said sum of _eight Dollars fifty Cents_ monthly for the term of _Ten_ months; the first payment to commence on the _first day of February 1801_

In witness whereof I have hereunto set my hand and seal the 14th day of November 1800

Jesse Cole

In presence and with the approbation of

Silas Talbot Captain.

Registered by

James P Deblois Purser.

Sailor's Allotment

Although many sailors went to sea to provide for their families, their absence meant the loss of a steady income until they returned. With mouths to feed and households to keep, women might take on small jobs to make ends meet; however, this was often not enough to cover expenses. Luckily, the Navy allowed sailors to sign an allotment like the one pictured here, giving half their monthly pay to their wives or children. This system helped sailors provide a small but steady income to their families until they returned home.

Allotment from Jesse Cole to his wife, Tabitha, 1801
Cole was a Seaman on board _Constitution_ from 1800-1801
Collection of the USS Constitution Museum, Boston

Did women join the crew?

Women were not allowed to join the Navy in 1812, but they did help in other ways, like supplying hand-sewn clothing needed for the ships' crews.

Despite being officially banned from American warships, there is evidence of a few cases of women on board Navy vessels.

- In 1803, there were at least five women on board USS *Chesapeake* - the wives of some of the junior officers, including the Captain of the Forecastle, the Gunner, the Boatswain, the Carpenter, and the Marine Corporal. One of them gave birth to a son in the Boatswain's storeroom.

- Two women, Mary Allen and Mary Marshall, were on board USS *United States* as nurses in May 1813.

- Surgeon Usher Parsons discovered a woman among the crew of USS *John Adams* in 1812 - she was disguised as a man!

Get History BUFF

MEET YOUR SHIPMATES

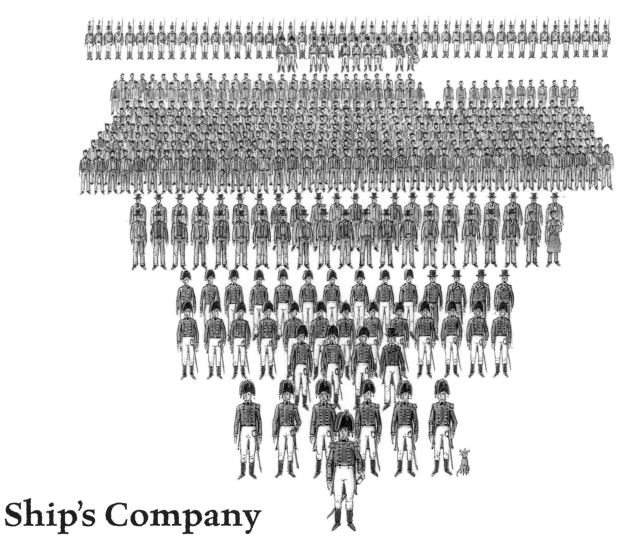

Ship's Company

Constitution was a massive and complex fighting machine, and it took 450 - 500 men to keep her at sea. Two thirds were sailors, and another 60 were Marines — naval soldiers.

The rest of the crew were officers. Just seven of them, the "commissioned" officers, were gentlemen-sailors who commanded the Ship. "Warrant officers" were naval tradesmen with special skills. Their assistants were called "petty officers."

Learn more about the lives of *Constitution*'s crew online! Click on the "Hands-on Activities" link on www.asailorslifeforme.org.

It is lonely at the top

As Captain, the responsibility for this great machine of wood, rope, and men ultimately rests on my shoulders. What I say is law. I have to make decisions based on what is best for the sake of ship and country, not individuals. The safety, well-being, and success of my men and our ship depend on my leadership.

Who am I?

I am Captain Isaac Hull from Derby, Connecticut. I first went to sea as a young boy on board merchant ships. When I was 26, I joined the Navy and became one of Constitution's lieutenants. Now, 13 years later, I stand here Captain of my favorite frigate.

Command the Crew

Try your hand at commanding a crew like Captain Hull.

How to play:

- Choose one person to be the Captain.
- Use tape or other objects to make a large outline of the deck of *Constitution* (see below).
- The Captain calls out commands from the list below that his or her crew must quickly follow. Crewmembers who don't follow the command are out!
- Go over all the commands before starting to make sure everyone knows what to do.

Commands:

- **"Captain's Coming!"**: The crew stops where they are and stands at attention with their feet together, arms at their sides, and standing up straight
- **"Man Your Boats!"**: The crew lines up single file in the middle of the ship area and pretends to row
- **"At Ease!"**: The crew stands with their feet apart and hands clasped together behind their backs
- **"Holystone the Deck!"**: The crew gets on their hands and knees and pretends to scrub the floor
- **"Seagull!"**: The crew ducks and covers their heads
- **"Crew to . . . "**
  - » **Starboard** (right) **side**
  - » **Port** (left) **side**
  - » **Bow** (front of the ship)
  - » **Stern** (back of the ship)
- **Add other commands, like "salute," "look through a telescope," "climb to the sails," etc. Be creative!**

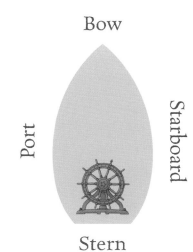

Bow

Port

Starboard

Stern

THE REAL THING

Officer's Sword

When dressed in full uniform, Captain Isaac Hull carried items reflective of his standing as an officer and a gentleman. Especially significant is his sword that hung on his left side. Captain Hull felt very connected to his sword. He could use it to defend himself if necessary, but it was more than a weapon, it was a symbol of what he had achieved.

Naval officer's dress sword owned by Isaac Hull, early 19th century
Hull was Captain on board *Constitution* in 1812
Collection of the USS Constitution Museum, Boston

In My Own Words

"I have now one of the best ships in our navy and a crew of 430 men, which you will think a large family, it's true; but being a good housekeeper I manage them with tolerable ease. I however scold sometimes and now and then get angry."

-Isaac Hull to Mary Wheeler,
July 12, 1810

Did you know?

Between 15 and 21 Midshipmen lived in a small space on the berthdeck called "steerage." Here the young officers slept, ate, wrote in their journals, and relaxed. With so many living in such a small area, steerage was a noisy, busy place.

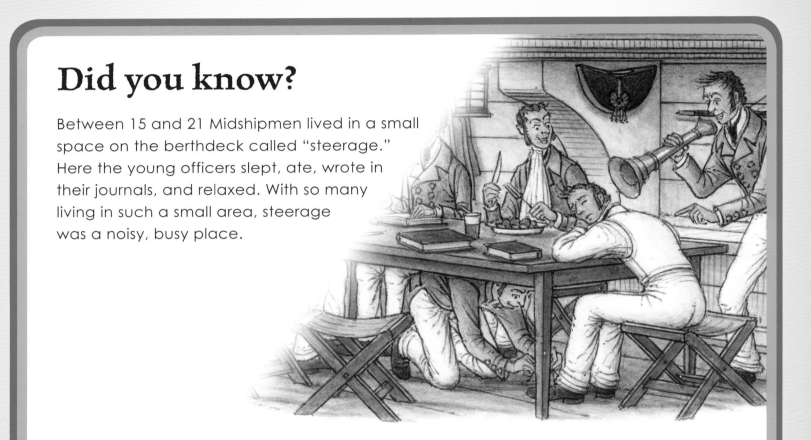

Who am I?

Probably the proudest day of my 22 years came when I, Pardon Mawney Whipple of Providence, RI, was appointed Midshipman and assigned to Constitution. My father, an officer in the Revolution, instilled in me a love for our young country and a belief that there is no greater honor than to fight for it.

Do you qualify to be a Midshipman in 1812?

- **Can you read and write?**

    NO - Sorry! You won't be able to perform your duties as a Midshipman without these skills.

    YES - Off to a good start! A Midshipman needs reading, writing, grammar, and penmanship skills to keep an official journal. Officers in training also need to know math and geography for navigation.

- **Do you have seafaring experience?**

    NO - That's okay! It's not required.

    YES - 58% of Midshipmen have previous seafaring experience.

- **Do you come from a coastal state?**

    NO - No problem. Midshipmen come from all regions of the United States.

    YES - The majority of Midshipmen come from Atlantic coastal states.

- **Are you between the ages of 12 and 18?**

    NO - That's all right. Boys younger than twelve and men over twenty can serve as Midshipmen.

    YES - You're in good company. The average age is 17.

- **Do you have a letter of recommendation from a senator?**

    NO - You will have to get one!

    YES - Good! Political and social connections are essential to gain an appointment as a Midshipman.

Even if you have all the qualifications necessary, your chances of becoming a Midshipman are only one in ten.

Keep a Logbook

Midshipmen had to keep a copy of the Ship's logbook. In each logbook entry, they recorded the date, weather, the Ship's location, and major events that happened that day.

Make your own logbook to record what's going on in your life!

You will need:

Paper

Pencil or pen

Outdoor thermometer (optional)

Compass (optional)

Make your logbook:

• Fold a few sheets of paper in half.
• Staple along the folded edge of the paper.
• Decorate the cover.

Date	Time	Weather	Location	What Happened Today

Write an entry:

Inside your logbook, write "Date," "Time," "Weather," "Location," and "What Happened Today" along the top of the page, as shown above.

• **Date:** Write the date.

• **Time:** Record the time.

• **Weather:** Take your logbook and pencil outside and observe the weather. What does it feel like outside? Is it sunny, rainy, or windy? Is it hot, cold, or somewhere in between? Write it down or draw a picture. If you have an outdoor thermometer, record the temperature.

• **Location:** Write down where you are right now.
  - If you have a compass, use it to figure out which direction you are facing. If you don't have a compass, you can describe where you are facing (for example, "I'm facing the front door of my house").
  - Describe a route you travel every day (such as the one between your house and your school) using landmarks. Landmarks can be stores or restaurants you know, mountains or lakes, or even funny colored houses.

• **What happened today**: Write down what you did today and what people in your family did today. Did you eat something special for lunch? Did you visit someplace new?

You have completed your first entry in your logbook. If you want to keep a logbook like Constitution's, write another entry tomorrow!

Become a Navigator

Part of the Midshipmen's education on board was navigation, or learning to determine *Constitution*'s location and direction at sea. How was this done with no land in sight? Well, each day Midshipmen measured the movement of celestial bodies – the sun, moon, or stars – using instruments like sextants or quadrants. They calculated the Ship's position using these measurements and mathematical tables.

Make your own navigation tool called a quadrant to measure the height of an object above the horizon.

You will need:

Protractor
Straw
String
Metal washer or three paper clips
Tape

Instructions:

Tie a washer or three paperclips to one end of the string. Tie or tape the other end of the string to the middle of the straight edge of the protractor, so that the string hangs down the center (at the 90 degree mark).

Tape the straw to the straight edge of the protractor, leaving a little space on either side. When you use the protractor, the straw edge will be on top.

Hold the protractor in your right hand (the numbers should be facing to your left). Look through the straw at the top of an object (like the moon, a star, a tall building, a tree, a telephone pole, or a mountain).

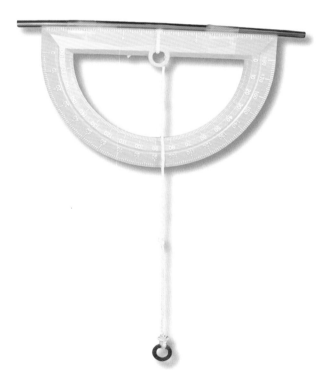

Have a partner look at the string and read the angle from the inner set of numbers on the protractor (0-90 degrees). Which angle degree does the string fall on? This will tell you the **zenith angle** (the angle between the highest point over your head [the zenith] and the object you're looking at). Subtract this number from 90 degrees to find the **altitude angle** (the height in degrees of the object above the horizon).

Try another object (it can be taller or shorter). Is this altitude angle larger or smaller?

Challenge! Try tracking the movement of a celestial body (like the moon or a star) over the course of a week. Each night at the same time, take a measurement of your object and calculate the altitude angle. How does it change over time? Why do you think it changes?

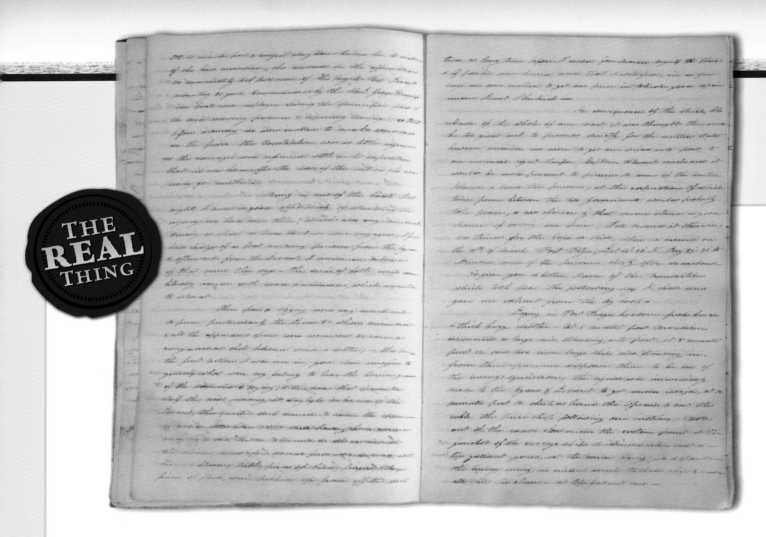

THE
REAL
THING

Not all of the Midshipmen's time was spent fighting the enemy or learning to be an officer. They had some time to spend as they pleased. When not enjoying the company of friends or reading, Midshipman Pardon Mawney Whipple recorded his experiences in this letterbook. He addressed each letter, "*Dear Friend.*"

In his first entry he wrote:

"I shall take a copy of my letters which will in some future day afford to myself the gratification of reviewing the scenes of past life – I shall make no further apology for my incorrect style, because you are well acquainted with the busy scenes of a seafaring life and the interruptions that so frequently occur, particularly onboard of a man of war."

Letterbook kept by Pardon Mawney Whipple, 1813-1821
Whipple was Midshipman on board *Constitution* from 1813-1815
Collection of the USS Constitution Museum, Boston

All for one and one for all

USS Constitution is a massive and complex fighting machine. It will take nearly 450 of us sailors working together as a team to achieve victory.

In My Own Words

"Constitution's crew was the smartest and her men the most capable ever known in the annals of history. Many of her men had been brought up on the sea, some had been masters of vessels both as sailors and marines and they were as united as brothers."

- Thomas Byron, Marine fifer on board USS Constitution, 1812

Did you know?

Historians estimate that, during the War of 1812, 7-15% of sailors in the Navy were free men of color.

Seafaring was one of only a few jobs that offered free African Americans a respectable career with equal pay.

Though racism wasn't absent at sea, free black sailors were integrated into the shipboard community - sleeping, eating and working side by side with their white counterparts.

Who am I?

I'm Jesse Williams. I've been to sea for a piece, and joined Constitution's crew as an Ordinary Seaman in August 1812. During battle, I'm one of the spongers on the third 24-pounder long gun. It's a dangerous job, but our crew practices until we can fire our gun with our eyes closed - we all have to work together to keep the Ship and each other safe!

EXPLORE

asailorslifeforme.org

Start your day off like a sailor . . . go online to scrub the deck! Click on the "Hands-on Activities" link on www.asailorslifeforme.org.

Holystoning

ENERGY

TOTAL TIME 00:16

SECTIONS LEFT 2

Quit Task

How do YOU compare to the average sailor in 1812?

- **How tall are you?**
  The average height was 5' 6".

- **How old are you?**
  The average age was 27 but a few were under 15 and over 50.

- **What color are your eyes?**
  The most typical eye color was gray (shade of blue).

- **What color is your hair?**
  The majority of sailors had brown hair worn short or tied back in a short queue (braid).

- **Are you African American?**
  7-15% of sailors were free men of color.

- **Do you have any tattoos?**
  5-10% of sailors had tattoos. Designs often included initials, anchors, hearts, or a cross.

- **Do you have any marks?**
  A seafaring life left many sailors with scars, burns, and missing fingers.

Get History **BUff**

MARINE

Did you know?

Prior to joining, about 40% of *Constitution*'s Marines worked as artisans or craftsmen, including butchers, bakers, blacksmiths, tailors, plasterers, shoemakers, silver platers, and coachmakers. Most of the other men were farmers or laborers before joining the Marines.

Who am I?

I, William Sharp Bush, grew up on the Eastern Shore of Maryland where I tried my hand at the business of farming. After my father died in 1809 I joined the Marine Corps and found my true calling. Now, three years later I am in charge of Constitution's Marine Guard.

Make a Marine Stock

As early as 1798, Marines wore a stiff collar of leather buckled around their necks. Called a "stock," this neckwear made the men keep their heads up and walk with a soldierly bearing. Even though the stock disappeared from the Marine uniform in 1872, the modern Marine Corps still refers to its men and women as "Leathernecks."

Make your own version of the Marines' "leatherneck."

You will need:

Paper
Scissors
Paint, markers, or crayons
String, ribbon, or an old shoelace

Instructions:

1. Draw an outline of a stock on a piece of paper. Use the examples on the next page as a guide.

2. Decorate your stock.

3. Cut out the shape.

4. Punch two small holes at each end of the stock.

5. Wrap the stock around your neck (the dip goes in front under your chin). Have someone thread the string or laces through the holes and tie them tightly in a bow.

Now you know what it feels like to be a Marine in 1812!

Use this shape as a guide

THE REAL THING

Musket

In port, *Constitution*'s Marines guarded the Ship with muskets like this. Before battle, some Marines climbed high onto a platform called a fighting top, where they fired down onto the decks of the enemy ship.

Springfield musket, 1811
Collection of the USS Constitution Museum, Boston

March Like a Marine

To be effective in battle, Marines learned to work and move together. Part of their training involved marching and turning as a group to the beat of a drum. Marines marched at the "common step." Each pace was two feet long, and they took 75 steps per minute. In addition, Marines were taught to point their toes as they marched.

Practice marching like a Marine!

• Gather a group and stand in a line. Each person should face the back of the person in front of him or her.

• The first person in line is the drill sergeant and will give the commands.

Commands:

• **"To the Front - March!":** Step off together with the left foot. Drill sergeant marks time by saying the cadence "Left… Left… Left, Right, Left" to make sure everyone steps on the proper foot at the proper time.

• **"Halt!":** Stop marching.

• **"To the Right - About Face!":** Turn in place 180 degrees clockwise. Face the way you came and march back to where you began.

• **"Company - Dismissed!":** Recruits may disperse!

The Female Marine?

In 1815, Boston printer Nathaniel Coverly published a best-selling <u>fictional</u> story about a woman named Lucy Brewer. After running away from home, Lucy disguises herself as a man, calls herself George, and enlists as a Marine on board *Constitution*. She survives the battle with HMS *Guerriere* and after a few years returns to her worried parents.

Readers liked the story so much that there were nineteen editions published between 1815 and 1818. Some of the editions changed Lucy's name to Louisa Baker, like the one pictured here.

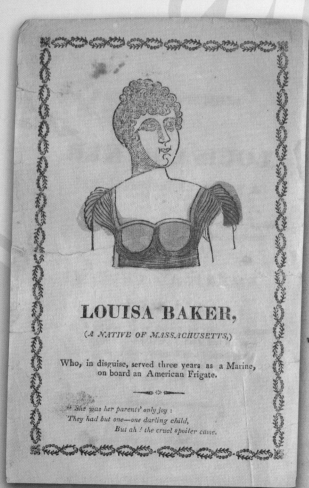

AN

AFFECTING NARRATIVE

OF

LOUISA BAKER,

A NATIVE OF MASSACHUSETTS,

WHO, IN EARLY LIFE HAVING BEEN SHAMEFULLY SEDUCED, DESERTED HER PARENTS, AND ENLISTED, IN DISGUISE, ON BOARD AN

AMERICAN FRIGATE

AS A MARINE,

WHERE, IN TWO OR THREE ENGAGEMENTS, SHE DISPLAYED THE MOST HEROIC FORTITUDE, AND WAS HONORABLY DISCHARGED THEREFROM, A FEW MONTHS SINCE, WITHOUT A DISCOVERY OF HER SEX BEING MADE.

PORTSMOUTH, N. H.
PRINTED FOR THE PURCHASER.
....1816....

Get History BUFF

"An Affecting Narrative of Louisa Baker," 1815
Collection of the USS Constitution Museum, Boston

GUERRIERE THE TERRIER

Woof!

I am a terrier, named Guerriere (it rhymes). Lieutenant Beekman Verplank Hoffman named me after Constitution's most famous opponent, HMS Guerriere. I am a favorite among the crew.

MEET YOUR SHIPMATES

Take a Trip with Guerriere

Download and print out "Flat Guerriere" and his accessories from the "Hands-on Activities" link on www.asailorslifeforme.org. Then, color and cut him out and bring him around your hometown, on family vacations, to school, or send him to friends and family and photograph his many adventures! Use a "Dog Log" to keep track of the terrier's travels and email the USS Constitution Museum (library@ussconstitutionmuseum.org) your favorite photo with a story of Guerriere's trip.

Dog Log

Date	Where did Guerriere visit?	What did Guerriere see?
8-19	Boston, Massachusetts	Guerriere returned to USS Constitution today. He was impressed to learn that the Ship is now the oldest commissioned warship afloat in the world.
8-19	Boston, Massachusetts	With dogged determination, Guerriere visited all the hands-on exhibits in the USS Constitution Museum. He gave his visit two enthusiastic paws up!

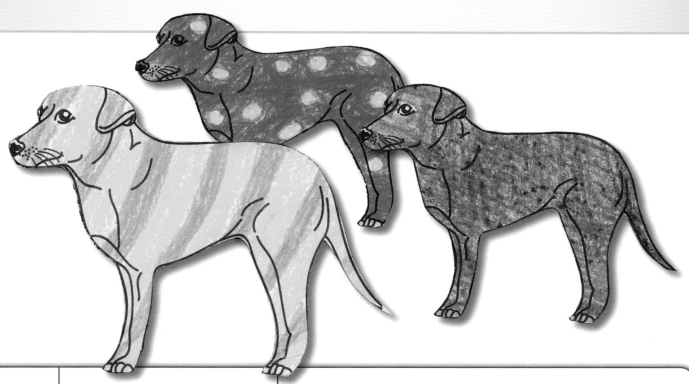

10-21	Portsmouth, England	Guerriere was right at home on HMS Victory – He saw lots about Admiral Nelson but not much about old sea dogs.
10-23	Paris, France	This was the highlight of Guerriere's Tour de France – the Eiffel Tower!

Hands-On Activity

Make Clothes for Guerriere

Sailor's Hat

Did you know?
This hat was very popular in 1812 and was worn by men on both land and sea.

Marine Cap

Did you know?
The Marine cap was called a "shako." The hats worn by marching bands today are based on the shako design.

Captain's Hat

Did you know?
The Captain's hat could fold flat and be carried under the arm.

Captain's Coat

Did you know?
The gold "shoulder pads" on the Captain's coat are called epaulettes and distinguished the Captain from the ship's lieutenants. Lieutenants wore one epaulette on their left shoulder, while the Captain wore two - one on each shoulder.

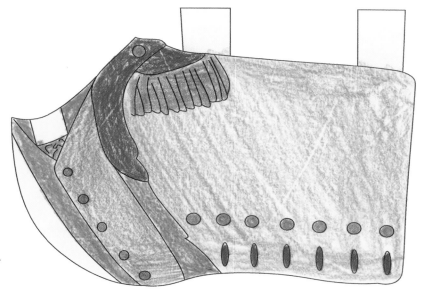

Listen to a Sea Chantey

Listen to an original chantey (sea-song) about Guerriere. Follow the lyrics to the chorus below and try to sing along.

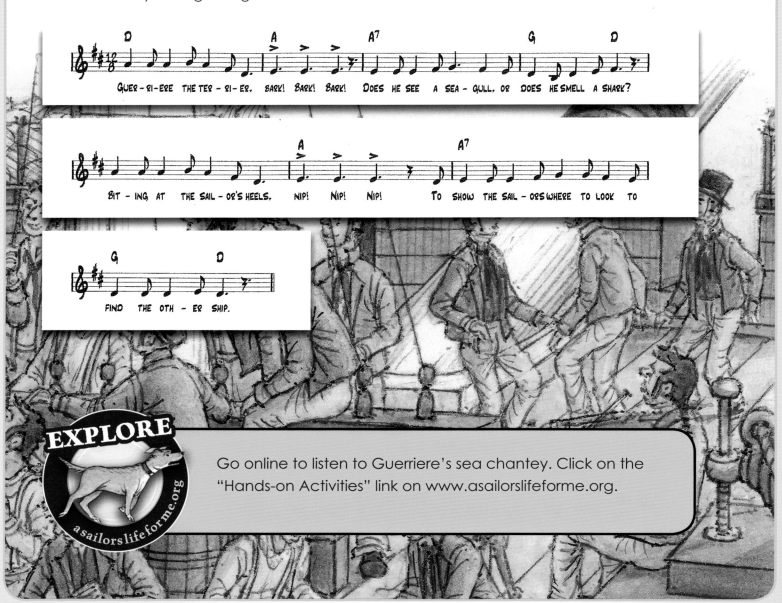

GUER-RI-ERE THE TER-RI-ER, BARK! BARK! BARK! DOES HE SEE A SEA-GULL, OR DOES HE SMELL A SHARK?

BIT-ING AT THE SAIL-OR'S HEELS, NIP! NIP! NIP! TO SHOW THE SAIL-ORS WHERE TO LOOK TO

FIND THE OTH-ER SHIP.

EXPLORE — a sailors life for me.org

Go online to listen to Guerriere's sea chantey. Click on the "Hands-on Activities" link on www.asailorslifeforme.org.

Did you know?

One day in February 1815, while standing on the Ship's rail, Guerriere began to bark. The sailors soon discovered that he was barking at a Portuguese ship on the horizon. The crew made ready for battle and, although the other ship proved friendly, Guerriere proved himself to be a helpful and intelligent sailor.

Guerriere is hiding from Lt. Hoffman. Head to the "Explore the Ship" section of www.asailorslifeforme.org to see if you can find him in 11 scenes.

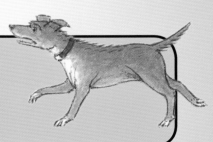

Make a Paper Dog

Step 1	
Fold a square piece of paper in half and open it back up.	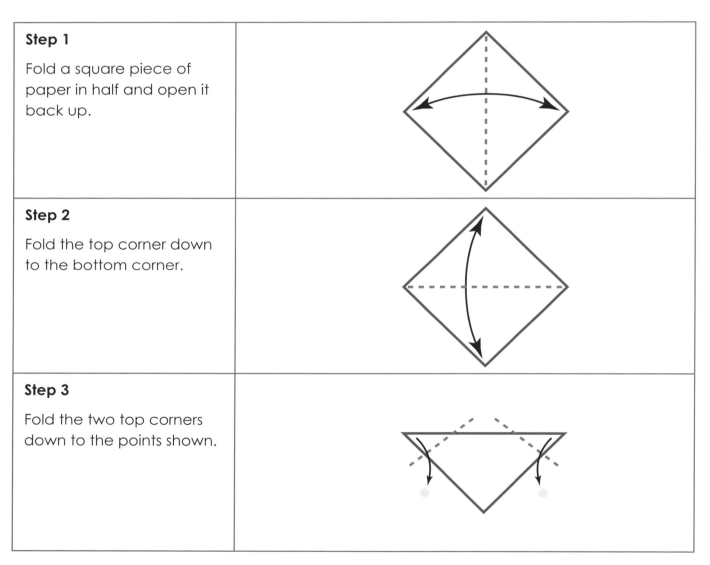
Step 2	
Fold the top corner down to the bottom corner.	
Step 3	
Fold the two top corners down to the points shown.	

Step 4	
Fold the top layer of the bottom corner up a little way.	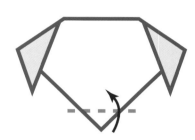
Step 5	
Fold this layer up again, from the top of the triangle as shown.	

Congratulations!
You've completed Guerriere. Now give him a personality and add eyes and a nose.

THE
REAL
THING

TIGERS.

THE Ladies and Gentlemen of *Worcester* and its vicinity,

are informed that

Two Royal Brazilian TIGERS,

Remarkably Elegant and Docile, taken by the U. S. frigate Constitution, out of the ship Susannah, will be Exhibited at *Capt Duncans Tavern on Friday Oct gant the 46*

To gratify the curiosity of those who may desire to see the
Monarchs of this Continent.

Admittance, 12 C

Two young "tigers," removed from a captured merchant ship, joined *Constitution*'s crew in 1814. When "Old Ironsides" returned to Boston in 1815 from another successful war cruise, the "tigers," like the Ship's sailors, became local celebrities. The animals were put on view for a fee in area taverns. This broadside advertises their appearance in Worcester, MA at Captain Duncan's Tavern, where the curious could see them for 12 cents.

Did you know?

These animals were described as "quite playful with the men, very tame and gentle, except when … eating." One of the Ship's cats fell victim to the "tigers" and a monkey on board just barely escaped.

Broadside, 1815
Courtesy of the American Antiquarian Society

Animals On Board *Constitution*

Guerriere wasn't the only animal on board *Constitution*. While officers brought chickens and goats for fresh eggs and milk, the sailors often took dogs and cats to sea. Occasionally there were even more exotic animals like squirrels, a raccoon, and at least one troublesome monkey who bit a sailor on the nose.

Get History BUff

ALL HANDS ON DECK

ALL HANDS ON DECK

Working Around the Clock

Sailors must be on deck to operate Constitution 24 hours a day. It is my job to divide the crew in half so sailors can take turns working and sleeping. Their day is divided into four-hour shifts, called watches. EVERYONE's job is interrelated and important.

	Middle Watch 12-4 am	Morning Watch 4-8 am	Forenoon Watch 8-12 noon
First Lieutenant	On Call: Sleep	Supervise crew, report progress to Captain	Receive reports that ship is clean and in proper order

Report to Captain when ready for inspection |
| **Midshipman** | On Call: Sleep | Supervise stowage of hammocks | Supervise cleaning of lower decks

Use a sextant to measure the sun's angle at noon |
| **Seaman** | Sleep | Scrub and dry decks, ladders, and hatches

Stow hammock | Breakfast

All hands on deck for training |
| **Boy** | Nap on deck unless needed | Sleep in hammock until 7:30

Stow hammock | Breakfast

Carry messages for officers

Gather for inspection |
| **Marine Private** | Sleep | Wash deck

Stand guard | Breakfast

Small arms practice |

Afternoon Watch **12-4 pm**	First Dogwatch **4-6 pm**	Last Dogwatch **6-8 pm**	First Watch **8-12 midnight**
Dinner 1:00 Get Purser's report about provisions	4:30 Evening quarters! Call men to their battle stations for inspection and practice	Go below Read book	On Call Sleep
Dinner 1:00 Learn naval tactics Write in journal	4:30 Attend evening quarters Inspect men in division	Help crew get hammocks down	Sleep
Dinner 12:00 Trim sails Perform routine maintenance	Supper 4:00-4:30 Attend evening quarters Practice sail or gun drill	Get hammock prepared Mess cooks receive salt meat for tomorrow's dinner	Sleep
Dinner 12:00 Mend clothes, nap, play with friends	Supper 4:00-4:30 Attend evening quarters Carry officers' messages Sweep deck	Nap, unless needed	Carry messages for officers
Dinner 12:00	Supper 4:00-4:30 Assemble for inspection and drill	Stand guard Set hammock down	Sleep

Did you know? Nobody knows for sure why the two half watches [from 4-6 and 6-8] are called dogwatches. Sailors like them because it keeps them from working the same shift every night.

LEARN THE ROPES

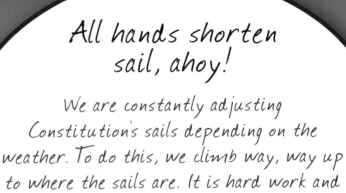

All hands shorten sail, ahoy!

We are constantly adjusting Constitution's sails depending on the weather. To do this, we climb way, way up to where the sails are. It is hard work and dangerous, especially at night. We can only do it if we work together as a team.

Learn the Ropes

Hands-On Activity Hands-On Activity Hands-On Activity

Tie a Knot

Sailors have to know how to tie many knots. See if you can learn the ropes.

You will need:

Two ropes (or shoe laces, or twine). Color one end red and the other blue

A straight object like a long wooden spoon, stick, or railing of a staircase

ALL HANDS ON DECK

Tie a Knot

Reef Knot (square knot)

One of the first knots sailors learned was a reef knot, necessary in shortening sail (reefing).

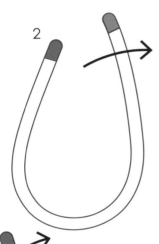

1. Hold the red end of the rope in your left hand and the blue end in your right.

2. Cross the red end over the blue end to create a loop.

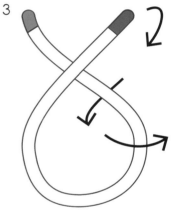

3. Pass the red end under the blue end and up through the loop.

4. Pull, but not too tight (leave a small loop at the base of your knot).

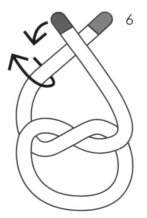

5. Hold the red end in your right hand and the blue end in your left.

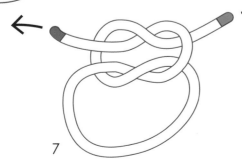

6. Cross the red end over and under the blue end and up through the loop (here, you are repeating steps 2 and 3)

7. Pull tight.

Clove Hitch

This knot "hitches" (ties) a line (rope) to a stationary object. In 1812, the crew of *Constitution* used hitch knots to attach ratlines (thin rope) to shrouds (thicker rope). The ratlines and shrouds were used as rope ladders to climb high up into the masts and rigging.

1. For this knot you will need an object like the handle of a long wooden spoon or a stick.

2. Hold your stick or spoon sideways.

3. Wrap the red end of the rope around the stick/spoon in one complete loop.

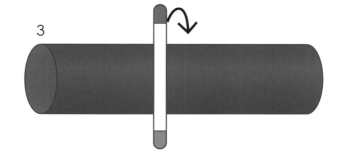

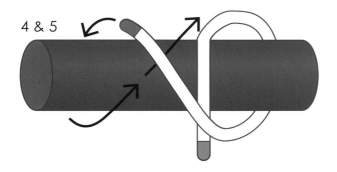

4. Cross the red end over the blue end.

5. Wrap the red end around the stick or spoon again.

6. Pull the red end of the rope up and through the loop that you just made. Pull tight.

Tie a Knot

Figure Eight

The figure eight knot is called a "stopper knot," because it prevents the end of a rope from being pulled through a block (pulley).

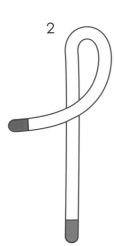

1. Hold the blue end of the rope in your left hand and the red in your right. The ends of the rope should be pointing down.

2. Cross the red end over the blue end to create a loop, as shown.

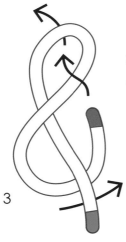

3. Pass the red end behind the blue end and down through the loop.

4. Pull tight.

Sheet Bend

This knot joins two ropes together.

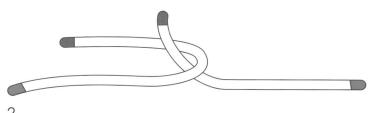

2

1. Hold the red end of one rope in your left hand and the red end of the other rope in your right.

2. Using the rope in your left hand, bend the red end around the red end of the rope in your right hand.

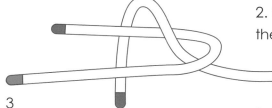

3

3. Pass the red end of the rope in your right hand behind the red and blue ends in your left hand.

4. Pass the red end of the rope in your right hand up and over the blue end in your left hand and under the center part of the rope in your right hand (this part can be tricky!)

4 & 5

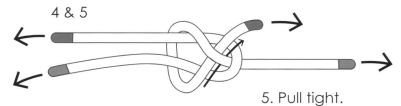

5. Pull tight.

Go online to help your shipmates haul on the lines to move the sails. Click on the "Hands-on Activities" link on www.asailorslifeforme.org.

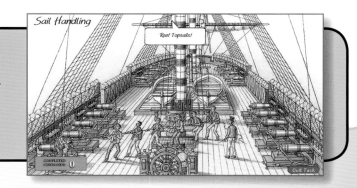

Tie a Knot

Bowline

The bowline knot (pronounced "bo-lin") is a loop knot, which means that it is tied around an object or tied when a temporary loop is needed. On *Constitution* in 1812, sailors used bowlines to haul heavy loads onto the Ship.

1. Hold the blue end of the rope in your left hand and the red end in your right.

2. Cross the red end over the blue end to make a loop.

3. Tuck the red end up and through the loop (pull, but not too tight!).

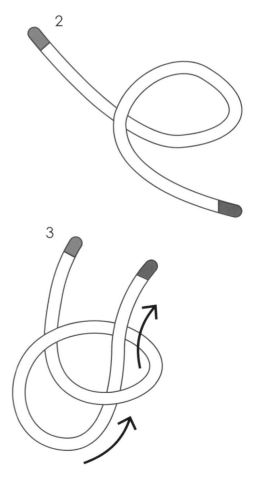

5 & 6

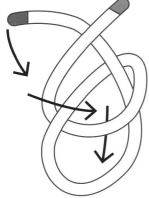

4. Keep the blue end of the rope in your left hand and the red in your right.

5. Pass the red end behind and around the blue end.

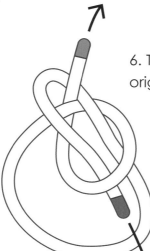

6. Tuck the red end down into the original loop that you made.

7. Pull tight.

7

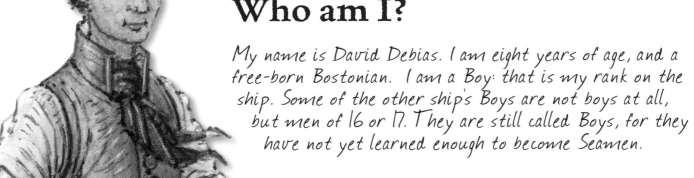

Who am I?

My name is David Debias. I am eight years of age, and a free-born Bostonian. I am a Boy: that is my rank on the ship. Some of the other ship's Boys are not boys at all, but men of 16 or 17. They are still called Boys, for they have not yet learned enough to become Seamen.

How many sailors fell from aloft?

Balancing on a footrope 150 feet above the water … at night … in a storm … during battle … was dangerous. On board *Constitution* during the War of 1812 there are four instances recorded of sailors falling from the rigging: none survived.

Get
History BUFF

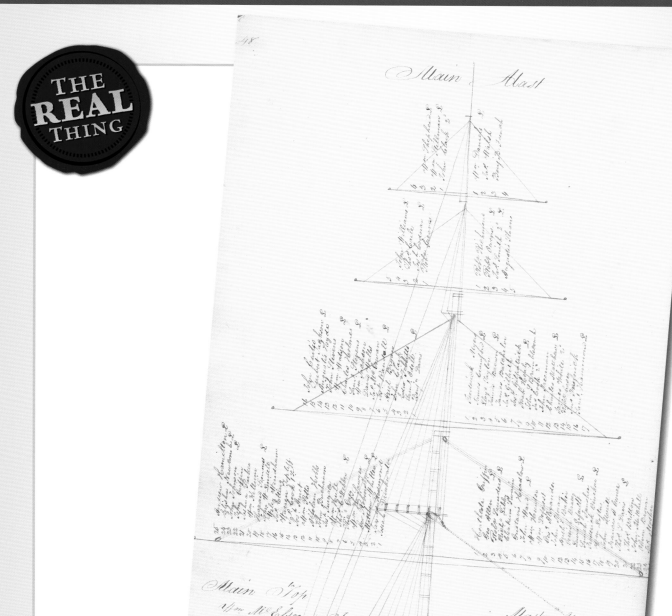

How many sailors did it take?

In 1827, *Constitution*'s First Lieutenant Elie Vallette drew each sailor's exact position aloft when the officer in charge ordered, "All hands to shorten sail."

Constitution Record Book kept by Elie Vallette, 1827
Vallette was Lieutenant on board *Constitution* from 1824-1828
Collection of the USS Constitution Museum, Boston

ALL HANDS ON DECK

Did you know?

Constitution almost sank in 1814! While sailing through a gale in the Bay of Biscay, the hawse plugs (stoppers for the holes where the anchor cable goes out of the ship) got knocked out by a huge wave, and tons of water rushed in. With orders from quick-thinking Lt. Shubrick, the crew stuffed hammocks in the holes and pumped the water out.

Painting of USF *President* at anchor in a storm by Antoine Roux, 1802; Courtesy of the Navy Art Collection, Naval History and Heritage Command

Go online to steer *Constitution* through narrow straits and shallow harbors to reach your destination. Click on the "Hands-on Activities" link on www.asailorslifeforme.org.

ALL HANDS ON DECK

Write a Secret Message

You will need:

Signal Flag Decoding Chart
Paper
Pencil
Markers, crayons, or colored pencils
Scissors
Yarn or string
A ruler or straight edge (optional)

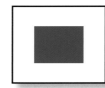 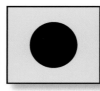

Instructions:

- Choose a word or phrase that you would like to spell (such as your name or a nautical word like "anchor," "ship," or even "USS Constitution").
- Using the Signal Flag Decoding Chart, find the flags that spell your word.
- Copy the flags that represent the letters in your words. Or, download and print them from the "Hands-on Activities" link on www.asailorslifeforme.org.
- Color and cut out your flags.
- String them together to create a word.
- Challenge your friends and family to decode your flags!

Signal Flag Decoding Chart

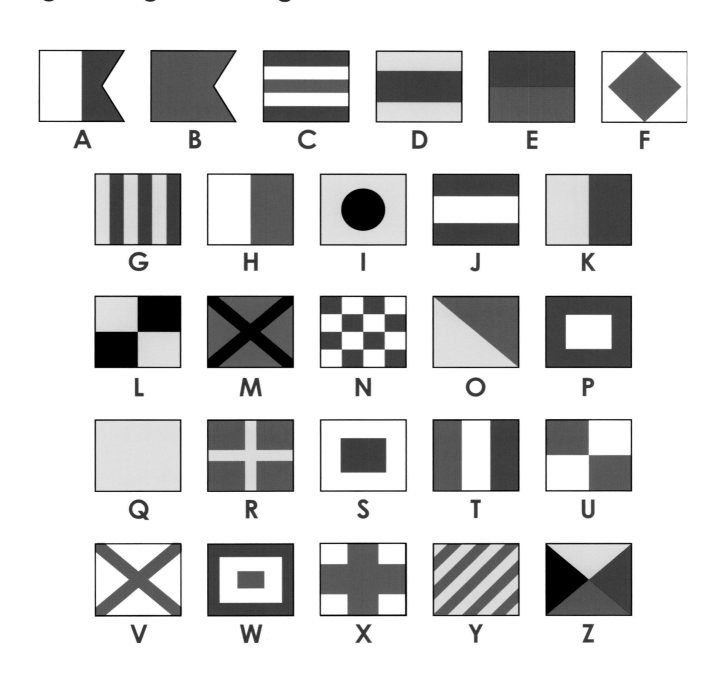

THE
REAL
THING

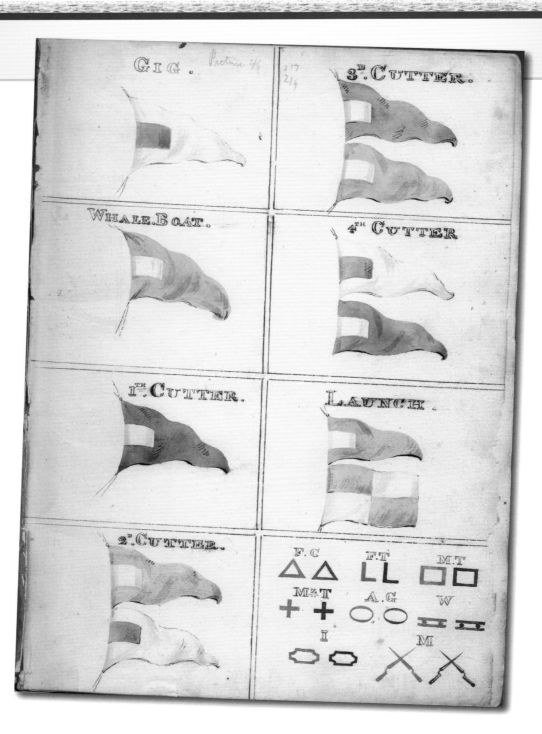

Ships used flags to communicate at sea. In 1827, Lt. Elie Vallette copied these signals into his journal. These colorful pennants were used to recall *Constitution*'s small boats back to the Ship.

Constitution Record Book kept by Elie Vallette, 1827
Vallette was Lieutenant on board *Constitution* from 1824-1828
Collection of the USS Constitution Museum, Boston

Did you know?

Signal flags were useless on a dark night. To communicate over long distances, ship captains used a combination of lanterns, flares (a rocket-like firework that burned red, blue, or white), or cannon fire.

Who am I?

Richard Dunn, here. I joined Constitution's crew at Annapolis, Maryland in 1812 as an Able Seaman. I am 25 years old and was born in Philadelphia. What do you think of my tattoo?

Cook a Sailor's Meal

I've gathered up some of my favorite recipes for you to try at home. They may taste and look different from what you're used to, but to a sailor who works hard all day, taste doesn't matter much.

Ship's Biscuit

Switchel

Hot Chocolate

Dandyfunk

Plum Duff

76

Cook a Sailor's Meal

Copy the recipes to cook your own sailor's meal. Or, download and print them out from the "Hands-on Activities" link on www.asailorslifeforme.org.

Ship's Biscuit

I serve this hard, bland bread on board every day. Sailors soak 'em in their stew or water before eating 'em. You should too. We don't want any broken teeth around here.

2 cups whole wheat flour
A little water
Baking sheet
Damp cloth

1. Preheat oven to 175 degrees.
2. Mix flour and enough water to form a stiff dough. If the dough is sticking to your fingers, add more flour. Cover with a damp cloth and let sit for ten minutes.
3. Fold and beat the dough until it is 1/2 inch thick. Repeat until dough is smooth.
4. Cut into circles, about 5 inches across. Pierce four times with a fork. Dust lightly with flour.
5. Place on ungreased baking sheet and bake for 3 hours, or until dry inside.

THE REAL THING

This ship's biscuit is REAL. A sailor kept it as a souvenir, writing "Constitution" and recording the date, 1861.

Why do you think a sailor saved this? Can you imagine saving a piece of bread today?

Ship's Biscuit issued on board *Constitution*, 1861
Courtesy of the Mariners Museum

Switchel

I mostly make this drink for the sailors during the summer months. The men love switchel because it tastes better than plain water and gives them more energy on a hot day.

5 cups water
1/2 cup vinegar
1/2 cup molasses
3 teaspoons ground ginger

1. Mix ingredients together in a bowl.
2. If it tastes too strong, add some water.
3. Serve cool and enjoy!

Hot Chocolate

Hot chocolate is a very popular drink with the crew. Sailors can buy chocolate from the Purser (the ship's storekeeper) for 37 cents a pound.

1 cup milk or water
2 tablespoons cocoa powder or 2 ounces semi-sweet or bittersweet chocolate
Sugar
Cinnamon (optional)
Chili powder (optional)
Vanilla (optional)

1. Heat the milk or water and stir in the chocolate until it's dissolved.
2. Remove the mixture from the stove, add sugar to taste, and froth it with a whisk.
3. Try adding different combinations of spices (or all of them) until you find your favorite!

Cook a Sailor's Meal

Dandyfunk

The sailors cook this up themselves when they can find some leftover ship's biscuit and get extra ingredients from me. They need the camboose (stove) to cook it, so they make sure to do it when I am not cooking.

1 piece of Ship's Biscuit (see Ship's Biscuit recipe) or 1 cup crushed, unsalted crackers
1 tablespoon vegetable shortening or lard
2 tablespoons dark molasses

1. Preheat oven to 350 degrees.
2. Put the biscuit or crackers into a plastic bag and crush into crumbs.
3. Mix crumbs with the shortening and add the molasses. Mix well.
4. Put mixture into a small, oven-safe dish.
5. Bake 15 minutes (or until it's brown and bubbling).

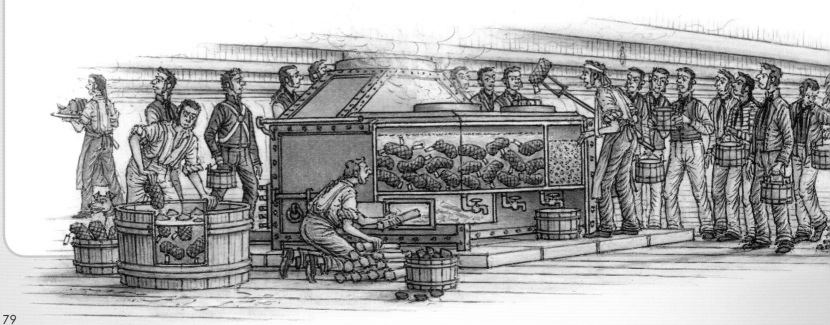

Plum Duff

Plum duff is another food that sailors can make for themselves. They have to be patient though; this doughy mixture takes four hours to cook.

2 pounds flour
1 pound shortening or lard
1/2 cup sugar
1/2 quart water
3/4 cup raisins
Cheese cloth
Kitchen string
Molasses

1. Bring a large pot of water to a boil.
2. Mix ingredients and knead the mixture with your hands, adding extra water if it's too dry.
3. Divide the mixture into four equal portions.
4. Wrap each portion in a piece of cheese cloth and tie at the top with a string.
5. Reduce the heat of the pot of water to medium-high.
6. Put the bags of cloth into the pot and boil for four hours. Serve with molasses.

Who am I?

I'm the cook, William Long. I was an Able Seaman once, but thanks to this wounded arm of mine I'm good for nothing. The Captain took me on board as cook, and the only battles I fight now are with beef, pork, and peas.

Did you know?

Mealtime was a sailor's favorite time of the day. The sailors who ate together (in a group called a mess) were like a family. They drank, laughed, and told stories. Messmates made the hard life of a sailor a little more pleasant. Their bond was strong and they always looked out for each other.

Unlike sailors, wardroom officers ate at tables and paid extra for fresher food that was cooked separately and served to them on china.

During the War of 1812, how much food did 450 sailors eat in six months?

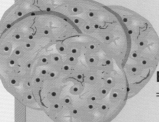

Bread: 84,456 lbs
= about 168,912 loaves of bread

Pork: 50,600 lbs
= about 338 pigs

Raisins: 360 lbs
= 3,840 small boxes of raisins

Beef: 57,700 lbs
= about 101 cows, or 230,800 hamburgers

Flour: 12,544 lbs
= about 209 bushels or the yield of 4 acres of land

Cheese: 2,174 lbs
= about 233 wheels of cheese

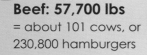

Butter: 1,765.5 lbs
= 7,062 sticks of butter

Suet (beef fat): 5,850 lbs
= fat from about 216 cows

Peas/Beans: 1,932 gal
= 13,738 16oz. bags

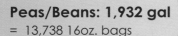

Rice: 1,657 gal
= 178 bushels or the yield of 4 ½ acres of rice

Vinegar: 1,310 gal
= 20, 960 8oz. cups

Molasses: 870 gal
= byproduct of 2 acres of sugar cane or 400,000 lbs of sugar cane

Sauerkraut: 800 gal
= about 4,000 cabbages and 2,400 tablespoons of salt

Spirits: 9,546 gal = 152,736 8oz. cups
Water: 47,265 gal = 756,240 8oz. cups

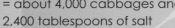 

82

Enjoy Free Time

Play a Dice Game

"Going to Boston" was a popular dice game on land and at sea. It's a simple game that can be played almost anywhere.

You will need:

3 dice
Paper and pencil
Cup (optional)

Players:

2-6 players

How to play:

- Roll the three dice. Set aside the die with the highest number.
- Throw the other two dice. Again, set aside the highest number.
- Throw the last die and set aside that number.
- Add up the three numbers and record your score.
- Pass the dice to the next player. Once everyone has had a turn, compare your scores – the player with the highest total wins the round.

Winning the game:

At the end of three rounds, compare your scores again – the player with the highest total wins the game!

Relax after a long day of work – go online to play a dice game or tell a tall tale with your shipmates. Click on the "Hands-on Activities" link on www.asailorslifeforme.org.

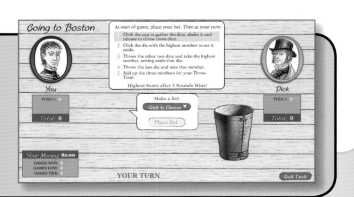

Hands-On Activity

Tell a Tall Tale

Sailors are known for spinning yarns (telling tall tales) about dramatic adventures they've had and outrageous things that they have seen.

Ask a friend to provide you with words to fill in the blanks in the following tall tales. Record the words on a separate sheet of paper. Then, read the story with the new words included.

You will need:

Paper
Pen or pencil

Story one

Now this terrible event took place when I was a (job), and our (adjective) (noun) was stranded in (location). We had not a breath of wind in a week, and one night a fog came down upon us. We knew that there was (something dangerous) all around us. What could we do? It was impossible to see from one side of the ship's (noun) to the other, and there was a (noun) dangerously close. Then I had a brilliant idea. I climbed the mast, cut up the fog with a sword, and tied it in a ditty bag with a (noun).

Cook served up portions of fog with gravy, and in two days we had eaten our way out to clear skies.

Story two

You might not believe this yarn, but I swear on my granny's grave that it's true. It was when our (adjective) (noun) was cruising in (adjective) seas in (location). I was standing in the ship's (room) when my parrot (name), who never usually left my shoulder, flew off and out of sight. He headed towards the (adjective) lands nearby, and I thought he was gone for good. So I was delighted when, just hours later, he returned – and with a leaf of purest gold in his beak! Of course I hid this from our (adjective) officers. The parrot repeated this trick the next day, and the one after. I would have been a rich man if our lousy, (adjective) ship's cat had not captured poor (parrot's name) and reduced him to a lifeless pile of brightly colored feathers.

Story three

I'm going to tell you an extraordinary story. It was back when I was a (job). We were cruising the (location) aboard a (noun) in the (adjective) seas off (adjective) coasts. We had turned (direction) to avoid a (hazard), when we suddenly heard a haunting song. There, sitting on a (noun) were three beautiful maidens. Their song instantly enchanted my (adjective) shipmates, who steered towards the rock. But I blocked my ears with (noun) and leaped from my position on the (location). I grabbed the helm, set a safe course, and tied the wheel with (noun). Then I fought off my shipmates until we were safely out of earshot.

To this day, I dream of those beautiful sirens every night.

THE
REAL
THING

Sailor's Powderhorn

Though designed to carry fine gunpowder, this powderhorn is a special memento of one sailor's service. Gunner John Lord made this in the 1820s. Using a technique called "scrimshaw" (carving or scratching designs into bone or ivory), Lord decorated this cow horn with images reflective of his proud service on board *Constitution*, including cannon and cannonballs, an anchor, a flag, and a scene of "Old Ironsides" in battle.

Powder horn decorated by John Lord, ca. 1824-1828
Lord was Gunner on board *Constitution* from 1824-1828
Collection of the USS Constitution Museum, Boston

Did you know?

Most sailors couldn't write their names. Officers had to be able to read and write, but common sailors didn't. Samuel Leech, a sailor in 1812, said that "many of my shipmates could neither read nor write…[and] were dependent on the kindness of others, to read and write for them." On board *Constitution* in 1813 only about one in five sailors could sign their name.

Obey Orders . . . or Else!

Cat-o-Nine-Tails

Seaman Moses Smith received six lashes with a cat-o-nine-tails for disobeying an officer's order. The humiliation of being tied to a grating and flogged in front of his shipmates was worse than the pain.

Cat-o-Nine-Tails, 19th century
Collection of the USS Constitution Museum, Boston

Did you know?

Whether sailing the ship or fighting an enemy, officers had to teach and maintain order and discipline among the crew.

In My Own Words

"Order is the first great principle on board a man-of-war. To this everything else must bend, and from it there is no appeal...."

- Charles Nordhoff, 1855

For those who did not obey orders, a variety of punishments awaited. For minor misdeeds, sailors might have their grog stopped or other special privileges revoked. For more serious crimes, a sailor could be arrested and handcuffed or struck with a cat-o-nine tails (whip).

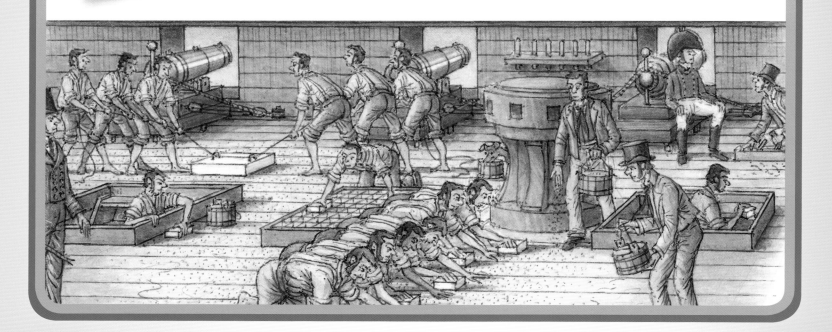

How often were sailors flogged?

The frequency of flogging varied by Captain. Flogging did not occur every day, but the threat of it was always present. When it did happen, all hands gathered to witness the punishment as a very powerful reminder of the officers' control over the sailors.

According to the surviving records, between 1812 and 1815 approximately 11 men were flogged for offenses ranging from desertion to smuggling liquor on board. During the same period, courts martial (military courts) awarded seven men between 50 and 100 lashes each for more grievous offenses such as theft and "mutinous behavior."

Get History BUFF

PREPARE FOR BATTLE

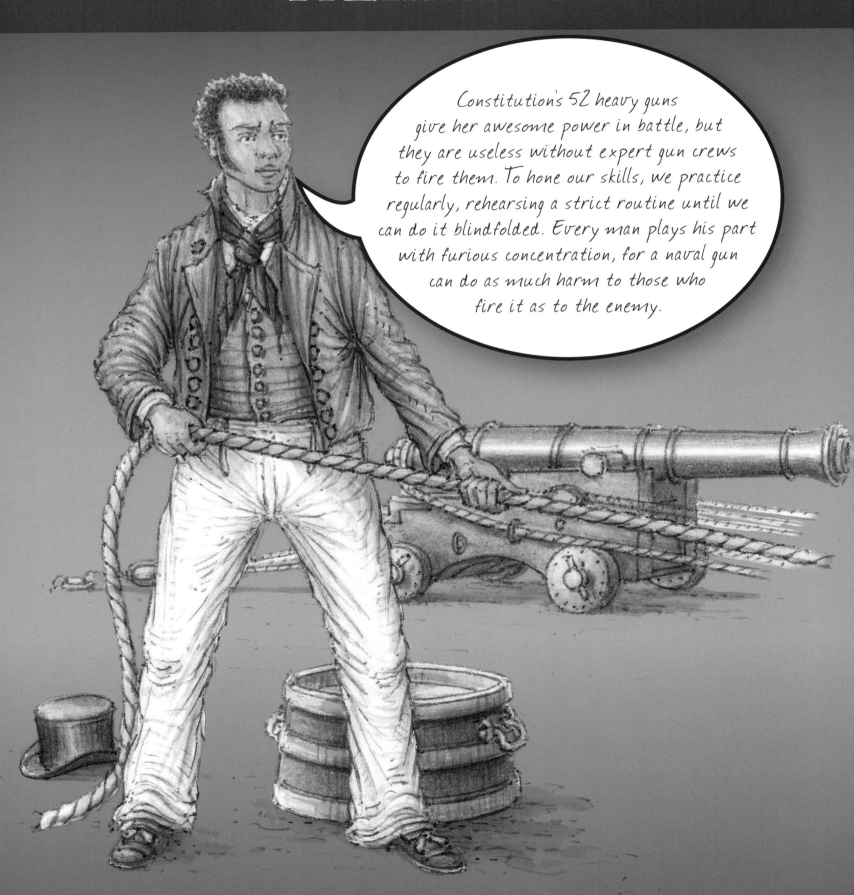

Constitution's 52 heavy guns give her awesome power in battle, but they are useless without expert gun crews to fire them. To hone our skills, we practice regularly, rehearsing a strict routine until we can do it blindfolded. Every man plays his part with furious concentration, for a naval gun can do as much harm to those who fire it as to the enemy.

Make and Fire Your Own Cannon

You will need:

An empty 35mm film container (or disposable salt or pepper shaker, or M&M's Minis® container [make sure the lid is not hinged to the container])

1-3 Alka-Seltzer® tablets

Warm water

Safety glasses (swimming goggles or sunglasses will work)

Note! Adult supervision required.

Test your cannon outdoors or somewhere you don't mind getting a bit wet.

Instructions:

1. Fill the film container 1/3 full with warm water (1/2 full for the salt shaker, and the M&M's Minis® container). Add 1/3 Alka-Seltzer® tablet (1 whole tablet for the salt shaker, and the M&M's Minis® container) and quickly pop the lid back on the film container.

2. Place the container (top up) on the ground and take five large steps back. Wait.

3. If it takes your cannon more than twenty seconds to fire, the adult should investigate.

4. Try the experiment again with different water temperatures or a different amount of Alka-Seltzer®. Does the speed or height of the reaction change? What about the "popping" noise?

Learn the Steps to Load and Fire a Cannon

During the War of 1812, it took 9 to14 well-trained men approximately two minutes to complete the 17 steps involved in firing a cannon. Below is a simplified version of those 17 steps.

1. **"Sponge your guns!"** Sailors use a wet sponger to extinguish any burning materials from the previous cannon fire.

2. **"Load your cartridge!"** A crewmember pushes a cloth bag filled with a pre-measured supply of gunpowder (called a "cartridge") down the cannon barrel with a tool called a rammer.

3. **"Shot your guns!"** The Gun Captain orders the loader to load a cannon ball (shot) into the cannon barrel and push it against the cartridge.

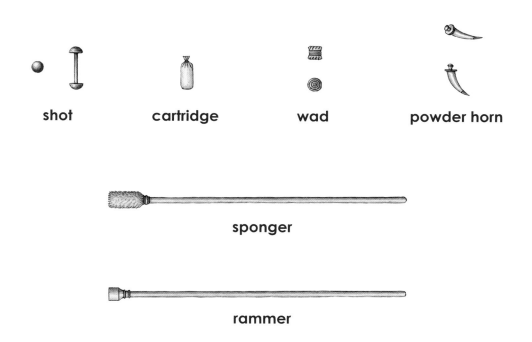

shot   cartridge   wad   powder horn

sponger

rammer

4. **"Wad to your shot!"** A sailor pushes a disc called a "wad" (often made of old rope) against the cannon ball to hold the shot in place.

5. **"Prime your guns!"** The Gun Captain pours a small amount of loose gunpowder from a powder horn into the touch hole.

6. **"Fire!"** A spark from the match or "flint lock" ignites the gunpowder in the touch hole. This powder burns and lights the cartridge on fire. The ignited cartridge explodes and pushes the shot out of the barrel. Huzza, the shot is fired!

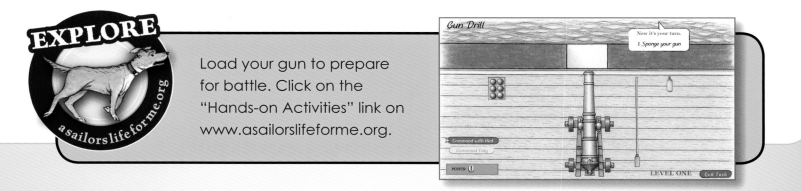

EXPLORE
asailorslifeforme.org

Load your gun to prepare for battle. Click on the "Hands-on Activities" link on www.asailorslifeforme.org.

SAIL TO VICTORY

A national ship

Our ship, USS Constitution, named for the country's founding document, built with American materials, and manned with sailors from across the nation, represents the whole country as we go into battle against Great Britain.

An enemy ship
has been spotted!

The drum beats, sending all hands to prepare for battle. In a flurry of activity we quickly ready the Ship for the fight. Breathlessly we hasten to our battle stations for the long painful wait. Hour after hour in tortured silence we contemplate our fate while we watch the enemy ship approach.

What do sailors feel as they wait for battle to begin?

Fear – Sailors worry that they or their friends might not survive the battle. What frightens you?

Excitement – The adrenaline pumps as the moment the sailors have been training for arrives. How do you feel when something you've waited for is about to happen?

Anxiety – Sailors are nervous because no one knows the outcome of the battle. What makes you anxious?

Illustration from the sketchbook of Lewis Ashfield Kimberly, 1857-1860
Kimberly was Lieutenant on board USS *Germantown* in the 1850s
Collection of the USS Constitution Museum, Boston

In My Own Words

"My pulse beat quick – all nature seemed wrapped in awful suspense – the dart of death hung as it were trembling by a single hair, and no one knew on whose head it would fall."

–Seaman David C. Bunnell, 1813

THE REAL THING

Gun Crew's Bible

As sailors waited for battle to begin, they were alone with their thoughts. They had time to dwell on the fear that they might never see their families again. Some gun crews strapped a Bible like this one to their cannon's carriage for extra protection.

Bible issued by the Bible Society of Nassau Hall, Princeton, New Jersey
Bible was strapped to the carriage of a gun nicknamed "Montgomery"
on board USS President, 1813
Collection of the USS Constitution Museum, Boston

EXPLORE

Go online to race the clock to bring powder to your cannon. Click on the "Hands-on Activities" link on www.asailorslifeforme.org.

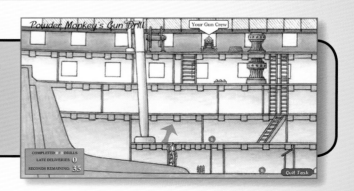

Powder Monkey's Gun Drill

Your Gun Crew

COMPLETED DRILLS
LATE DELIVERIES 0
SECONDS REMAINING 35

Quit Task

SAIL TO VICTORY

What are the characteristics of a brave sailor?

Courage – Sailors push fear aside to do their job. What have you done that took courage?

Responsibility – Each sailor has to do his duty to his country, ship, and shipmates. What are your responsibilities to your community, school, or family?

Team Player – Working together is critical to succeed in battle. How do you work or play as part of a team?

In My Own Words

"We're so close (to HMS Guerriere) we can see the whites of the eyes and count the teeth of the enemy.."

-Seaman Moses Smith, 1812

USS *Constitution* vs. HMS *Guerriere*

Follow Captain Isaac Hull's diagram and read his descriptions of the battle that made *Constitution* famous.

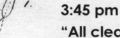

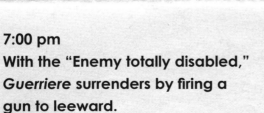

3:45 pm
"All clear for action" *Constitution*'s crew shortens sail and runs out the guns, ready for battle.

6:20 pm
". . . in less than fifteen minutes from the time, we got alongside [firing broadside after broadside], his Mizen Mast went by the board . . ."

6:30 pm
As the two ships collide, marines prepare to board *Guerriere* "but the instant the Boarders were called … his Foremast, and Mainmast went by the board."

7:00 pm
With the "Enemy totally disabled," *Guerriere* surrenders by firing a gun to leeward.

Isaac Hull's Battle Diagram, 1821; Private collection

Get History **BUFF**

Play Battle It Out

The object of the game

It is August 19, 1812 - USS *Constitution* and HMS *Guerriere* face off in battle 600 miles off the coast of Boston. Refight this historic battle to see which ship can outgun its opponent and sail to victory.

You will need:

Battle It Out game board (in back pocket or download from the "Hands-on Activities" link on www.asailorslifeforme.org)

2 playing pieces (select two pieces from another game or use buttons, coins, etc)

2 dice
1 coin
Pencil and paper to keep score

Getting started:

Divide the players into two teams. One team will be playing for the United States Ship *Constitution*, and the other for the British Ship *Guerriere*.

Each team selects a playing piece and places it on their start space. The American team moves along the blue track, and the British team moves along the red track.

Playing the game:

To Move: When it's your team's turn, roll the dice and advance that number of spaces ahead.

To Fire: If you land on a space in a firing zone where your opponent is, your team can fire its ship's guns. Firing is only permitted when both ships are in the same zone at the same time.

To get a hit in the...

Short-range firing zone: Flip a coin once. If you get heads, you've scored a hit.

Long-range firing zone: Flip a coin twice. If you get heads both times, you've scored at hit.

Keep track of how many hits each team earns.

Bonus hit: If you land on a white space and your opponent is on an adjacent square you get an automatic hit.

Winning the game: The ship that is first to hit its opponent six times is the winner.

Did women participate in battle?

On board the British ship *Guerriere* women helped carry the powder to the guns (cannon). *Constitution* sailor Moses Smith witnessed this and wrote, "The women they had with them were engaged in passing powder, and other munitions of war. Amid such activity on the decks of the enemy, courage and prudence demanded that we should be active on our own."

Get History BUFF

Ready ... Aim ... Fire! Go online to lead your gun team to victory. Click on the "Hands-on Activities" link on www.asailorslifeforme.org.

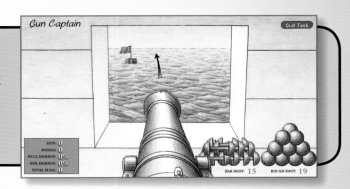

How USS *Constitution* earned the nickname "Old Ironsides"

On August 19, 1812, USS *Constitution* engaged HMS *Guerriere* in an epic battle. Amidst the deafening roar and choking smoke of cannon fire, a sailor watched as cannonballs bounced off *Constitution*'s thick wooden sides. In amazement, he cried out, "Huzza, her sides are made of iron!" Ever since, the Ship has been affectionately known as "Old Ironsides."

Get History BUFF

EXPLORE
a sailors life for me.org

Go online to watch *Constitution* battle it out during the War of 1812. Click on the "Hands-on Activities" link on www.asailorslifeforme.org.

Draw the Missing Moment

For 200 years artists have depicted *Constitution*'s battle against HMS *Guerriere*, like the series of paintings below by George Ropes, Jr. None have illustrated the defining moment when the Ship earned her nickname, "Old Ironsides." Help fill in the gap in the historic record by making your own drawing of that missing moment.

"Huzza! Her sides are made of iron!"

"Constitution and Guerriere" by George Ropes, Jr., 1813
Collection of the USS Constitution Museum, Boston

Who am I?

I am called Amos Evans, though the men know me instead as "Saw-Bones." I learned medicine from Ben Rush, one of our nation's greatest physicians. My love of the sea led me to become a navy surgeon's mate in 1808 (though I might have earned four times more ashore). After two years I was promoted to full surgeon, and I sailed with Constitution in June 1812.

In My Own Words

"'You are a hard set of butchers,' was all I said to the surgeon, as my torn and bleeding limb was severed from my body."

– Seaman Richard Dunn,
August 20, 1812

Bone Saw

This bone saw is a surgeon's tool of last resort. He uses it to remove the mangled leg or arm of a wounded sailor. The sailor is awake during the operation so a good surgeon cuts with great speed. After battle, the surgeons from the two ships work together to ease the suffering of all the wounded.

Bone Saw from the Surgeon's Medical Chest owned by William Swift, early 19th century
Swift was Surgeon on board USS *Chesapeake* during the War of 1812
Courtesy of the Massachusetts Historical Society

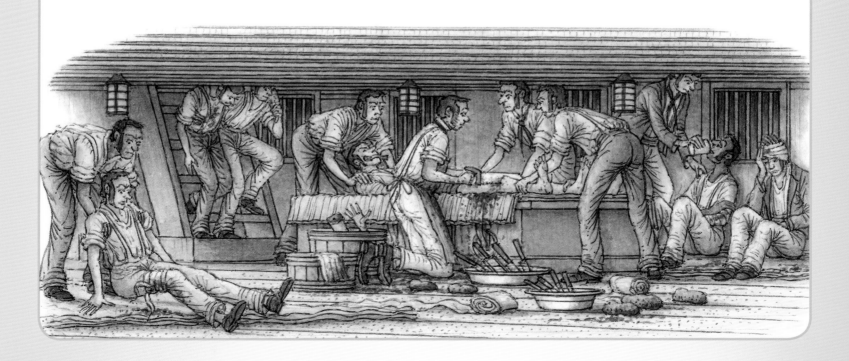

What do sailors feel after battle?

Compassion – Sailors show concern for those injured during the battle. How do you show compassion?

Horror – Sailors are shocked to see the destruction caused by their guns. How do you feel when your words or actions hurt someone?

Pride – Sailors feel a sense of accomplishment after winning the battle. How do you feel when you win something?

In My Own Words

"I do not mind the day of battle, the excitement carries one through; but the day after is fearful; it is so dreadful to see my men wounded and suffering."

– Captain Isaac Hull, 1812

RETURN HOME

A ship becomes a symbol

After USS *Constitution*'s string of surprising victories over the British during the War of 1812, Americans no longer saw "Old Ironsides" as an ordinary warship. Instead, the Ship became a symbol of the country's strength and proof that the young nation would succeed.

In My Own Words

"She has been a good friend to many a worthy tar and carried them through long and perilous cruises and done more honor to herself than any other ship in the Navy."

- Midshipman Pardon Mawney Whipple, 1814

In My Own Words

"Let us keep Old Iron Sides at home. She has, literally, become a Nation's ship, and should be preserved in honorable pomp, as a glorious monument of her own, and our other naval victories."

- National Intelligencer May 23, 1815

Presentation Urn

Captain Isaac Hull's success in the *Guerriere* battle made him a national hero. A grateful nation presented him with gifts like this silver urn made by Thomas Fletcher and Sidney Gardiner.

Silver Urn presented by the citizens of Philadelphia to Captain Isaac Hull, 1813
Made by Thomas Fletcher and Sidney Gardiner, Philadelphia, 1813
Private collection

Sing a Victory Song

The song depicted here was printed shortly after *Constitution*'s victory over HMS *Guerriere* on August 19, 1812. Set to the tune of "Yankee Doodle" it celebrates the brilliant naval victory when *Constitution* earned the nickname "Old Ironsides" and became a national symbol.

This song was sung in taverns across the country. Give it a try and sing along. Create your own song set to the tune of "Yankee Doodle" to celebrate an important moment in your family's life.

Go online to listen to another song sung in taverns to celebrate *Constitution*'s victory. Click on the "Hands-on Activities" link on www.asailorslifeforme.org.

THE AMERICAN

CONSTITUTION FRIGATE'S

ENGAGEMENT WITH THE BRITISH FRIGATE GUERRIERE,

Which after an Action of 25 Minutes, Surrendered, and being completely Shattered, was blown up, it being impossible to get her into port.

COME jolly lads, ye hearts of gold,
  Come fill your cans and glasses,
Be fun the order of the day,
  A health to all our lasses.
    Yankee doodle keep it up,
    Yankee doodle dandy,
    As hot as British folks can sup,
    We'll give it to 'em handy.

The Constitution long shall be
  The glory of our Navy,
For when she grapples with a foe.
  She sends her to old Davy.
    Yankee doodle keep it up,
    Yankee doodle dandy,
    We'll let the British know that we
    At fighting are quite handy.

Not long ago Five British Ships
  Unto her gave a chace sir,
But spite of all their quips and cranks
  She beat 'em in the race, sir.
    Yankee doodle, keep it up,
    Yankee doodle dandy,
    Though ten to one, the Yankee boys
    At fighting are quite handy.

At length the British ship Guerriere,
  Quite proudly came across her,
And Dacres said, in half an hour,
  In air he'd surely toss her.
    Yankee doodle, keep it up,
    Yankee doodle dandy,
    He counted chickens ere they hatch'd,
    Because the eggs were handy.

But soon, alas! poor Dacres, found
  That he was quite mistaken,
And thought he got himself well off,
  By saving of his Bacon.
    Yankee doodle, keep it up,
    Yankee doodle dandy,
    The Yankee boys for fighting fun,
    Are always quick and handy.

And now begun the bloody fray,
  The balls flew thick and hot sir,
In half an hour the job was done,
  The Guerriere went to pot sir.
    Yankee doodle, keep it up,
    Yankee doodle dandy,
    The British did'nt like the fun,
    And quit soon as 'twas kandy.

Now here's a health to CAPTAIN HULL,
  And all his noble crew sirs,
And should he choose to fight again,
  His lads will see him through sirs.
    Yankee doodle, keep it up,
    Yankee doodle dandy,
    For riddling British ships I'm sure,
    Brave HULL is quite the dandy.

Now safe in Boston port we're moor'd,
  Our girls with smiles shall meet us,
And every true American,
  With loud huzzas shall greet us.
    Yankee doodle, keep it up,
    Yankee doodle dandy,
    Our brave commander now we'll toast,
    In punch, and wine, and brandy.

"The American *Constitution* Frigate's Engagement with the British Frigate *Guerriere*" Broadside, c.1812
Collection of the USS Constitution Museum, Boston

What happened to the sailors?

USS *Constitution*'s sailors returned victorious three times during the War of 1812. Sailors enjoyed their success and received extra pay called prize money. Eventually, they returned to their ordinary lives with just the memory of an extraordinary moment.

Not all sailors were so lucky. Some were injured in battle, and others didn't return at all.

William Bush

Lewis Bush learned of his brother's death in a letter:

"[William Bush] mounted the taffrail, sword in hand and as he exclaimed 'Shall I board her' received the fatal ball in his left cheek... Thus fell that great and good officer who when living was beloved & now gone is deeply regretted by his country & friends but he died as he lived, with honor to both." - John Contee, Lt. Marines, September 13, 1812

A descendant of Lewis Bush carried this letter with him while serving in World War II to gain strength from the memory of his brave ancestor. The letter is now in the collection of the USS Constitution Museum.

David Debias

I joined *Constitution*'s crew at the tender age of eight. At thirty-two I was serving as a sailor on a merchant ship when it stopped at a port in Alabama. Although born free in the North, officials there suspected I was a runaway slave and imprisoned me. Every day is a nightmare as I wait for proof of my Navy record to arrive and I am free again.

A lawyer sent a letter to the Secretary of the Navy pleading Debias' case and requesting that his Navy record be sent to his captors as proof that he was not a slave. The Secretary of the Navy responded, confirming his naval service and status as a free man.

Richard Dunn

I suffered a terrible wound in my leg during the battle with *Guerriere* and the surgeon sawed it off. Because of this, I received a lifetime pension of $6.00 per month and Captain Hull collected $1,000 in donations for me. And for the next 25 years, he found me work at every navy yard he commanded.

Dunn died at age 76 on February 1, 1863.

Pardon Mawney Whipple

Serving in the Mediterranean in 1821 I rescued ten sailors from storm-toss'd boats. Though these deeds brought me some glory, I now realize they were rash because – perhaps as a result – I contracted the Wasting Disease. This has ended my service in the Navy, and I fear may also end me.

Whipple's worst fears came true when he died from tuberculosis in 1827 at the age of 37. In his will, Whipple left his French books and his shell and mineral collection to his sweetheart, Eliza.

Jesse Williams

I helped *Constitution* earn victories over *Guerriere* and *Java*. Later I fought in the successful Battle of Lake Erie for which my state of Pennsylvania awarded me a medal. My luck ran out while assigned to USS *Scorpion*. The British captured us and we became prisoners of war until the peace treaty was signed.

Williams received the equivalent of 2 1/2 years of wages in prize money. He slips out of history after 1830, when he was living alone in Strasburg Township, Pennsylvania.

Play the *Constitution* Challenge

Are you ready for a promotion? Test your seafaring knowledge to find out.

You will need:

Constitution Challenge game board (in back pocket or download from the "Hands-on Activities" link on www.asailorslifeforme.org)

List of questions (Go to the "Hands-on Activities" link on www.asailorslifeforme.org to print the questions needed)

1 die

Playing pieces (select pieces from another game or use something you have around the house such as buttons or coins)

How to play:

Put player pieces on the "start" square.

The youngest player goes first.

After rolling the die, move the appropriate number of spaces forward.

Depending on the roll, a player will land on either chance spaces or yellow spaces.

- **Chance spaces** are the squares with images and directions. Example, "For bravery in battle, roll again."
- **Yellow spaces** require answering a question.
  - » The person to the right of the player reads a question.
  - » If the question is answered correctly, the player moves ahead one space.

To get promoted and win the game:

The winner of the game is the one who lands on the end square first with an exact roll.

Did you know?

USS *Constitution* is the oldest commissioned warship afloat in the world. Launched in Boston in 1797, she saw service in the Quasi War with France, the Barbary Wars, and the War of 1812, emerging with an undefeated record. In 1997, in honor of the 200th anniversary of her launch, *Constitution* sailed under her own power for the first time in 116 years. She was made America's Ship of State in 2009. Today, you can visit USS *Constitution* in Boston, MA year round!

Visit the Ship's website at:
www.history.navy.mil/ussconstitution/

The **USS Constitution Museum** is an award winning museum that invites visitors of all ages to participate in the story of "Old Ironsides" through hands-on exhibits and dynamic programming. Come swing in a hammock, fire a cannon, furl a sail, or scrub a deck to see if a sailor's life is for you. Located next to USS *Constitution* in Boston, the Museum is open daily.

Go to www.ussconstitutionmuseum.org to plan your visit.